The Wealth of Purpose: Transforming Passion into Prosperity

By: J. R. Glenn

Copyright: 2024

Table of Contents:

Table of Contents:
- **Chapter 1: Understanding Purpose**
  - **The Concept of Purpose**
  - **The Importance of Knowing Your Why**
  - **Purpose as a Driving Force**
- **Chapter 2: The Power of Passion**
  - **Identifying Your Passion**

- Passion vs. Hobby: Understanding the Difference
- The Role of Passion in Wealth Creation

Chapter 3: Purpose-Driven Entrepreneurship
- Defining Purpose-Driven Business
- Case Studies of Successful Purpose-Driven Entrepreneurs
- Building a Business Aligned with Your Values

Chapter 4: Cultivating a Wealth Mindset
- Understanding Wealth Beyond Money
- Shifting Your Mindset for Abundance
- Overcoming Limiting Beliefs

Chapter 5: Personal Branding and Identity
- Crafting Your Unique Brand
- Aligning Your Brand with Your Purpose
- The Impact of Authenticity on Success

Chapter 6: Purposeful Living and Minimalism
- Defining Minimalism in the Context of Purpose
- The Benefits of Simplifying Your Life
- Creating a Purposeful Environment

Chapter 7: Financial Independence through Passion Projects
- Identifying Viable Passion Projects

- Strategies for Monetizing Your Passions
- Balancing Passion Projects with Financial Goals

Chapter 8: Spiritual Wealth and Personal Growth

- The Intersection of Spirituality and Wealth
- Practices for Nurturing Spiritual Wealth
- Personal Growth as a Wealth Builder

Chapter 9: Goal Setting and Achievement Strategies

- Setting Purpose-Driven Goals
- Effective Strategies for Achieving Goals
- The Role of Accountability in Success

Chapter 10: Legacy Building and Impact Investing

- Understanding Legacy Beyond Financial Wealth
- Strategies for Impact Investing
- Creating a Lasting Legacy through Purpose

Chapter 11: Work-Life Balance and Fulfillment

- Defining Work-Life Balance
- Strategies for Achieving Balance
- The Connection Between Purpose and Fulfillment

Chapter 12: Emotional Intelligence and Wealth Creation

The Role of Emotional Intelligence in Success

  Developing Emotional Awareness

  Leveraging Emotional Intelligence for Wealth

Chapter 13: Building Your Purpose-Driven Community

  The Importance of Community Support

  Networking with Purpose-Driven Individuals

  Collaborative Projects for Shared Goals

Chapter 14: The Journey of Continuous Growth

  Embracing Change and Adaptability

  Lifelong Learning as a Path to Wealth

  Celebrating Your Progress and Future Goals

Resources:

Chapter 1: Understanding Purpose

The Concept of Purpose

The concept of purpose serves as a cornerstone for understanding not only who we are but also the pathways we choose in life. It encapsulates the driving force behind our actions, informing our decisions and shaping our identities. When individuals embark on the journey to discover their "why," they often find that purpose transcends mere ambition; it is the essence of what fuels their passions and aspirations. By aligning our pursuits with a deeper sense of purpose, we can cultivate a wealth mindset that encourages both personal and financial growth. This alignment is crucial in transforming passion into prosperity, as it provides the foundation upon which meaningful achievements are built.

Purpose-driven entrepreneurship epitomizes the intersection of personal values and business ventures. Entrepreneurs who are clear about their purpose are more likely to create products and services that resonate with their target audience. This authenticity not only differentiates them in a competitive marketplace but also fosters a loyal customer base. When business owners operate with a clear sense of purpose, their ventures evolve into platforms for impact, allowing them to channel their passions into financial independence. This approach empowers them to navigate challenges with resilience and creativity, as their purpose serves as a guiding star during turbulent times.

Embracing a wealth mindset involves cultivating an understanding that true wealth extends beyond monetary gain. It encompasses emotional intelligence, personal growth, and the ability to live life with intention. Individuals who prioritize purpose in their lives are often more fulfilled, as they engage in work that aligns with their values and aspirations. This fulfillment not only enhances their emotional well-being but also positions them to become influential leaders in their communities. By focusing on purposeful living and minimalism, they can declutter their lives, allowing space for what truly matters, thereby enriching their overall experience and satisfaction.

Goal setting and achievement strategies are significantly more effective when grounded in a clear sense of purpose. When individuals establish goals that resonate with their values and passions, they are more motivated to pursue them relentlessly. The alignment of goals with purpose creates a sense of direction, enabling individuals to allocate their resources—time, energy, and finances—more effectively. This intentional approach to goal setting fosters a cycle of achievement that reinforces the individual's sense of purpose, creating a positive feedback loop that enhances both personal and professional growth.

Legacy building and impact investing are natural extensions of a purpose-driven life. Individuals who understand their "why" are better equipped to create a lasting impact, both in their personal lives and in the lives of others. By investing in causes and projects that reflect their values, they contribute to a broader narrative of wealth that includes social and environmental considerations. This holistic view of wealth encourages a balanced approach to life, promoting work-life harmony and fulfillment. Ultimately, by centering their lives around purpose, individuals not only enrich their own experiences but also leave a meaningful legacy that inspires future generations.

The Importance of Knowing Your Why

Understanding the significance of knowing your "why" is a transformative step toward living a life of purpose and fulfillment. Your "why" serves as the foundation of your identity, guiding your decisions, shaping your goals, and determining your path in life. It is the intrinsic motivation that fuels your actions, whether in personal endeavors or entrepreneurial pursuits. By identifying and embracing your "why," you create a strong anchor in an often chaotic world, enabling you to navigate challenges with resilience and clarity.

In the realm of purpose-driven entrepreneurship, knowing your "why" distinguishes successful ventures from fleeting trends. Entrepreneurs who align their business objectives with a deeper purpose often inspire loyalty and engagement from customers and employees alike. This alignment fosters a culture of authenticity, where stakeholders are not just invested in the product but also in the mission behind it. As a result, businesses rooted in purpose can drive innovation, attract like-minded individuals, and ultimately achieve sustainable growth.

A wealth mindset is intricately linked to understanding your "why." When you recognize the personal reasons behind your aspirations, you cultivate a more profound sense of motivation and commitment to your goals. This mindset encourages you to view challenges not as obstacles but as opportunities for growth. By focusing on your purpose, you can reframe setbacks as learning experiences, enhancing your emotional intelligence and capacity for wealth creation. A purpose-driven approach ensures that your pursuit of financial independence is not merely about accumulating wealth but about achieving a meaningful legacy that reflects your values.

Personal branding and identity are also deeply influenced by knowing your "why." In a world saturated with information and competition, having a clear purpose helps you stand out. It allows you to authentically communicate your values and vision, creating a brand that resonates with others. By articulating your "why," you can attract a community that shares your beliefs and aspirations, fostering connections that enhance both personal and professional growth. This authenticity cultivates trust and reliability, essential components in building a strong personal brand that withstands the test of time.

Ultimately, leading a purposeful life requires consistent reflection and alignment with your "why." It serves as a compass in your journey toward work-life balance and fulfillment. By regularly revisiting and refining your understanding of your purpose, you can make informed choices that enhance your emotional well-being and contribute to your overall prosperity. Embracing a minimalist lifestyle can further support this endeavor, allowing you to focus on what truly matters and eliminate distractions that hinder your progress. By committing to a life driven by purpose, you not only enhance your own journey but also create a positive impact on those around you, leaving a lasting legacy that extends beyond financial success.

Purpose as a Driving Force

Purpose serves as a fundamental driving force in our lives, shaping our actions, decisions, and ultimately, our sense of fulfillment. When individuals seek to understand their "why," they embark on a journey of self-discovery that can lead to profound transformations in both their personal and professional spheres. Identifying a clear purpose not only enhances motivation but also provides a compass for navigating the complexities of modern life. This sense of direction is crucial for those aiming to align their passions with their pursuits, creating a harmonious balance between personal satisfaction and financial success.

In the realm of purpose-driven entrepreneurship, having a well-defined purpose can significantly influence business outcomes. Entrepreneurs who understand their core values and the impact they wish to create are more likely to attract like-minded customers and partners. These individuals often find that their passion fuels their business, leading to innovative solutions and a loyal customer base. By fostering a culture of purpose within their organizations, they can inspire employees, enhance productivity, and contribute to a more meaningful work environment that benefits everyone involved.

Embracing a wealth mindset is another critical aspect of understanding purpose as a driving force. This mindset encourages individuals to view wealth not solely in financial terms but as a broader concept that includes emotional, spiritual, and social dimensions. When people recognize that their purpose can drive wealth creation, they begin to see opportunities where others may only perceive obstacles. This shift in perspective empowers individuals to pursue their passion projects with vigor, ultimately leading to financial independence and a more enriched life.

Personal branding and identity are intricately linked to one's purpose. When individuals articulate their unique value proposition based on their passions and purpose, they create a powerful narrative that resonates with others. This narrative not only sets them apart in a competitive marketplace but also attracts opportunities that align with their goals. By cultivating a strong personal brand rooted in purpose, individuals can enhance their visibility and influence, paving the way for greater achievements and meaningful connections.

Lastly, the pursuit of a purposeful life often emphasizes the importance of legacy building and impact investing. People who are clear about their purpose tend to focus on creating lasting change and contributing to the greater good. This long-term vision encourages them to invest their time, resources, and talents in initiatives that align with their values, ultimately leaving a positive mark on the world. By integrating purpose into their financial strategies and life choices, individuals not only enrich their own lives but also inspire others to embrace a similar path of fulfillment and impact.

Chapter 2: The Power of Passion

Identifying Your Passion

Identifying your passion is a crucial step in discovering your purpose, which in turn acts as the foundation for a fulfilling and prosperous life. Passion serves as the driving force that energizes individuals, motivating them to pursue their goals with enthusiasm and determination. To effectively identify your passion, start by reflecting on the activities that bring you joy and fulfillment. Consider moments when you lost track of time because you were so engrossed in what you were doing. These experiences often reveal the areas where your true interests lie and can serve as a compass for your journey toward aligning your life with your purpose.

Another effective strategy for identifying your passion is to examine your strengths and skills. Often, the things we are naturally good at can provide insight into what we may enjoy doing. Take inventory of your talents and consider how they can be applied to various pursuits. This alignment between passion and skill not only enhances your ability to succeed but also contributes to a sense of fulfillment. Engaging in activities that leverage your strengths can create a synergy that propels you forward, allowing you to cultivate your passion into something more substantial.

Additionally, seeking feedback from those around you can offer valuable perspectives. Friends, family, and colleagues can often see qualities and interests in you that you might overlook. Engaging in conversations about your aspirations and interests can spark new ideas and lead to insights that help clarify your passions. This collaborative approach not only deepens relationships but also fosters an environment where you feel supported in your quest for purpose. The insights gained from others can serve as a guide, illuminating paths you may not have considered on your own.

Exploring new experiences is another vital aspect of discovering your passion. Stepping outside your comfort zone and trying new activities or hobbies can uncover hidden interests. Whether it's volunteering, taking a class, or attending workshops, immersing yourself in diverse experiences can ignite a passion you didn't know existed. This exploratory mindset encourages growth and allows you to connect with like-minded individuals, further enriching your journey. Embracing new opportunities can lead to unexpected paths that align with your purpose and contribute to your overall sense of wealth.

Finally, it is essential to remember that identifying your passion is not a one-time event but a continuous process. As you evolve, your interests and values may shift, requiring you to reassess what drives you. Embrace this fluidity and remain open to change as you navigate your path. Cultivating a mindset of curiosity and reflection will enable you to adapt and find joy in your pursuits. By actively engaging in this process, you can transform your passions into a powerful vehicle for achieving not just financial independence, but a deeply fulfilling and purpose-driven life.

Passion vs. Hobby: Understanding the Difference

Passion and hobby often intertwine in the fabric of our daily lives, yet they serve distinct purposes that can profoundly affect our personal and professional journeys. Understanding the difference between the two is crucial for those seeking deeper meaning and fulfillment. A hobby is typically an activity pursued for enjoyment and relaxation, often without the expectation of financial gain or long-term commitment. It provides a pleasurable escape from the rigors of daily life and can be a source of leisure and social interaction. However, while hobbies enrich our lives, they may lack the intrinsic motivation that drives lasting engagement and purpose.

Passion, on the other hand, is a powerful force that fuels one's ambitions and aspirations. It goes beyond mere enjoyment; it embodies a deep-seated commitment to a cause or activity that resonates with one's core values and identity. Passion is often accompanied by a desire to excel, contribute, and make a meaningful impact in the world. When you are passionate about something, the energy and dedication you invest can lead to transformative experiences and outcomes, both personally and financially. This distinction is vital for anyone striving to discover their "why" in life, as understanding one's passions can illuminate the path toward purpose-driven entrepreneurship and financial independence.

In the realm of purpose-driven entrepreneurship, recognizing the difference between passion and hobby can help individuals align their business ventures with their core values. Entrepreneurs who harness their passions often find themselves more resilient in the face of challenges, as their drive stems from a profound connection to their work. This connection not only enhances their emotional intelligence but also nurtures a wealth mindset, fostering a culture of innovation and meaningful engagement. By focusing on passion rather than merely treating a venture as a hobby, individuals can create sustainable businesses that reflect their unique identities and aspirations.

Moreover, passionate pursuits can facilitate personal growth and spiritual wealth. Engaging in activities that ignite one's passion encourages self-reflection and goal setting, allowing individuals to uncover their true potential. This journey of exploration often leads to a clearer understanding of one's legacy and impact on the world. When passion intersects with purpose, it cultivates an environment ripe for achievement and fulfillment, promoting a balanced and meaningful life. As individuals align their passions with their broader life goals, they begin to cultivate a lifestyle that prioritizes well-being over mere financial success.

Ultimately, distinguishing between passion and hobby is essential for anyone looking to build a life of purpose and prosperity. By embracing their passions and integrating them into their daily lives, individuals can embark on a transformative journey toward financial independence and legacy building. This understanding allows for a more intentional approach to work-life balance, ensuring that every endeavor contributes to personal fulfillment and wealth creation. As you explore your own passions, remember that they are not just activities to fill your time; they are the keys to unlocking a richer, more purposeful existence.

The Role of Passion in Wealth Creation

Passion serves as a vital catalyst in the journey of wealth creation, influencing not only financial success but also personal fulfillment. When individuals pursue their interests and passions, they often discover unique opportunities that align with their skills and values. This alignment fosters a deep sense of purpose, which can significantly enhance motivation and perseverance. In contrast to pursuing wealth for its own sake, engaging with passion-driven pursuits encourages a holistic approach to life, integrating emotional and spiritual richness into the fabric of one's endeavors.

Understanding the connection between passion and wealth creation begins with recognizing the intrinsic motivation that passion ignites. Passionate individuals are more likely to invest time and energy into their projects, leading to innovation and resilience in the face of challenges. This commitment often translates into improved performance, whether in business or personal ventures. A wealth mindset rooted in passion encourages individuals to view obstacles as opportunities for growth, fostering a proactive approach to problem-solving that is essential for long-term success.

Furthermore, purpose-driven entrepreneurship exemplifies the powerful intersection of passion and economic success. Entrepreneurs who create businesses based on their passions not only contribute to the economy but also pursue work that resonates with their core values. This authenticity resonates with customers and clients, fostering loyalty and long-term relationships. As these entrepreneurs grow their businesses, they often create a ripple effect, inspiring others to pursue their passions, thus contributing to a larger culture of purpose-driven living.

Personal branding and identity are also significantly enhanced when passion is at the forefront. Individuals who align their personal brands with their passions create a compelling narrative that attracts like-minded communities and opportunities. This not only enhances their visibility in their chosen fields but also solidifies their position as thought leaders. By being true to their passions, they cultivate a sense of authenticity that resonates with others, establishing a legacy that extends beyond financial wealth to include influence and inspiration.

Ultimately, the pursuit of financial independence through passion projects is a testament to the transformative power of aligning one's work with personal values. Passion-driven endeavors often yield not just monetary rewards but also a profound sense of fulfillment and purpose. By embracing the interplay of passion and wealth creation, individuals can build lives that are not only successful in financial terms but also rich in meaning and legacy. This holistic approach to wealth encourages a balance between professional aspirations and personal well-being, nurturing a life of abundance in every sense.

Chapter 3: Purpose-Driven Entrepreneurship

Defining Purpose-Driven Business

Defining a purpose-driven business involves understanding the core motivations that propel individuals and organizations towards meaningful and impactful outcomes. At its essence, a purpose-driven business transcends the traditional profit-centric model, embedding a deeper significance into its operations. This approach aligns closely with the personal journeys of individuals seeking their "why" in life, as it emphasizes the importance of passion and values in shaping business endeavors. For those who are exploring their purpose, recognizing how a business can reflect personal beliefs and aspirations is crucial in creating a fulfilling and financially sustainable venture.

Purpose-driven entrepreneurship is characterized by a commitment to making a positive impact on society while simultaneously pursuing financial success. This dual focus not only attracts like-minded individuals and customers but also fosters loyalty and trust, which are essential for long-term success. Entrepreneurs who embed their personal reasons into their business strategies often find themselves more motivated and engaged. This engagement translates into higher productivity, creativity, and resilience, which are vital traits for overcoming challenges in the business landscape. By identifying and articulating a clear purpose, entrepreneurs can forge a path that is both profitable and personally rewarding.

The wealth mindset coaching framework can be instrumental for individuals seeking to develop a purpose-driven approach to entrepreneurship. This coaching emphasizes the importance of aligning one's financial goals with personal values and passions. It encourages individuals to shift their focus from mere monetary gain to creating value that resonates with their identity. As individuals embrace this wealth mindset, they begin to see opportunities not just as potential income sources, but as avenues for personal growth and community impact. This transformation can lead to a more profound sense of fulfillment and financial independence, as passion projects evolve into sustainable businesses that reflect the essence of the entrepreneur.

Building a strong personal brand rooted in purpose is essential for those looking to navigate the complexities of modern entrepreneurship. A purpose-driven identity allows individuals to communicate their values clearly and authentically, attracting customers and collaborators who share similar beliefs. This alignment fosters a supportive community that reinforces the individual's mission and enhances business credibility. As entrepreneurs cultivate their personal brands, they also contribute to a culture of purposeful living, where minimalism and intentionality play significant roles. This approach not only reduces distractions but also sharpens focus on what truly matters, creating a more balanced and fulfilling life.

Lastly, emotional intelligence emerges as a key component in the realm of wealth creation within purpose-driven business. Understanding one's emotions and the emotions of others can significantly enhance decision-making, leadership, and relationship-building. Entrepreneurs equipped with emotional intelligence are better positioned to navigate the challenges of their journeys, fostering a work-life balance that promotes well-being and fulfillment. By embracing this holistic approach, individuals can create a legacy that reflects their values and impact, ensuring that their pursuit of financial success is intertwined with a commitment to positive change and personal growth.

Case Studies of Successful Purpose-Driven Entrepreneurs

Case studies of successful purpose-driven entrepreneurs provide not only inspiration but also practical insights into the transformative power of aligning personal passion with business ventures. One notable example is Blake Mycoskie, the founder of TOMS Shoes. Mycoskie created a company with a mission to provide a pair of shoes to a child in need for every pair sold. This "one for one" model not only resonated deeply with consumers but also turned TOMS into a globally recognized brand. Mycoskie's commitment to social responsibility exemplifies how a clear purpose can lead to both financial success and positive social impact, demonstrating that business can indeed be a force for good.

Another compelling case is that of Yvon Chouinard, the founder of Patagonia. Chouinard has built his brand around a deep commitment to environmental sustainability, with initiatives that prioritize responsible sourcing and activism. Patagonia's mission statement, which emphasizes the preservation of the planet, has attracted a loyal customer base that values ethical business practices. This dedication to purpose has not only cultivated a strong brand identity but also has positioned Patagonia as a leader in the outdoor apparel industry. Chouinard's journey illustrates that aligning business practices with personal values can create a lasting legacy and foster a community of like-minded individuals.

Marie Forleo, an entrepreneur and author, also exemplifies the impact of purpose-driven pursuits. Through her platform, she empowers individuals to pursue their passions and develop their unique skills. Her commitment to helping others achieve personal growth reflects a larger philosophy that success is intrinsically tied to the contributions one makes to society. Forleo's ability to blend her passion for coaching with entrepreneurial ventures showcases how a clear sense of purpose can lead to financial independence while enriching the lives of others. Her story emphasizes the importance of identifying one's "why" as a foundation for creating meaningful work.

The case of Warby Parker further illustrates how purpose-driven entrepreneurship can disrupt traditional industries. The eyewear company was founded with the goal of providing affordable glasses while also addressing the issue of vision impairment in developing countries. For every pair of glasses sold, Warby Parker donates a pair to someone in need. This dual commitment to customer satisfaction and social responsibility has not only driven sales but has also redefined consumer expectations in the eyewear market. Warby Parker's success highlights how purpose-driven business models can attract customers who seek to make a difference through their purchases.

Finally, consider the journey of Elon Musk, who has consistently pursued ventures that align with his vision of advancing humanity. Whether through Tesla's push for sustainable energy or SpaceX's mission to make life multiplanetary, Musk's entrepreneurial endeavors are deeply rooted in a desire to address global challenges. His approach to business emphasizes that wealth creation is not solely about financial gain but also about making a significant impact on the world. Musk's story is a powerful reminder that purpose-driven entrepreneurship can transcend traditional boundaries, leading to groundbreaking innovations that foster both economic growth and societal advancement.

Building a Business Aligned with Your Values

Building a business aligned with your values starts with a deep understanding of what those values are. This process often involves introspection and self-discovery, where individuals examine their beliefs, passions, and motivations. When you clarify what truly matters to you, it becomes easier to craft a business model that reflects these principles. Consider what drives your passion and how those elements can be woven into your entrepreneurial endeavors. This alignment not only enhances personal satisfaction but also fosters authenticity in your brand, attracting customers who resonate with your mission.

As you embark on this journey, it's essential to recognize the importance of purpose-driven entrepreneurship. Businesses built on a foundation of strong values tend to foster loyalty among customers and employees alike. This loyalty translates into long-term relationships, which are invaluable for sustainable growth. By prioritizing purpose over profit, you create a compelling narrative that differentiates your business in a crowded marketplace. Emphasizing your values can attract like-minded individuals to your cause, creating a community centered around shared beliefs and goals.

Financial independence can also stem from passion projects that align with your values. When you merge your business endeavors with what you love, work no longer feels like a chore. Instead, it becomes a source of joy and fulfillment. This sense of purpose can drive you to overcome obstacles and challenges that may arise along the way. When you are deeply connected to your work, you are more likely to innovate and push boundaries, leading to opportunities for growth that may not have been apparent otherwise.

In addition to personal fulfillment, building a values-driven business can significantly impact your legacy. Your business can serve as a vehicle for change, influencing not only your life but also the lives of others. By integrating impact investing and socially responsible practices into your model, you can create a ripple effect that extends beyond your immediate sphere. This commitment to making a positive impact can attract investors and partners who share your vision, further reinforcing the importance of purpose in your entrepreneurial journey.

Lastly, it is crucial to maintain a balance between your values and the operational aspects of your business. This requires emotional intelligence and a keen awareness of how your decisions align with your core beliefs. Emphasizing work-life balance and fulfillment is essential to avoid burnout and ensure that you remain connected to your purpose. Regularly revisiting your values can help you stay grounded, guiding your decisions and keeping your business aligned with your true self as you navigate the dynamic landscape of entrepreneurship.

Chapter 4: Cultivating a Wealth Mindset

Understanding Wealth Beyond Money

Understanding wealth transcends the mere accumulation of money; it encompasses a broader spectrum of value that includes purpose, fulfillment, and personal identity. For individuals seeking their "why" in life, recognizing that wealth can be derived from passion-driven endeavors is crucial. This perspective invites a shift from traditional views of success defined solely by financial metrics to a more holistic understanding that values emotional intelligence, personal growth, and legacy. Wealth becomes more than a number; it transforms into a reflection of one's values, contributions, and the impact one has on the world.

Purpose-driven entrepreneurship exemplifies this concept, showcasing how businesses can thrive when anchored in a mission that resonates deeply with the founder's values. Entrepreneurs who align their ventures with their passions often find that the rewards extend beyond profits; they build communities, foster connections, and inspire others. This aligns closely with the idea that wealth is about creating meaningful experiences and cultivating relationships. By focusing on purpose rather than just profit margins, individuals can achieve a sense of fulfillment that financial gains alone cannot provide.

Moreover, a wealth mindset fosters resilience and adaptability, qualities essential for navigating the challenges of purposeful living. Embracing a mindset that prioritizes growth and learning enables individuals to see obstacles as opportunities for personal development. This approach not only enhances one's emotional intelligence but also reinforces the belief that true wealth is multifaceted. As people cultivate their skills and pursue their passions, they often discover new avenues for financial independence, creating a sustainable model where their work aligns with their beliefs and values.

Personal branding and identity play a significant role in understanding wealth beyond money. When individuals articulate their unique narratives and align their personal brands with their intrinsic values, they attract opportunities that resonate with their purpose. This alignment fosters authenticity, allowing individuals to connect deeply with others who share similar values and aspirations. In this way, wealth is not only about what one possesses but also about who one becomes and the legacy one leaves behind.

Finally, the journey toward wealth that encompasses personal growth, emotional fulfillment, and purposeful living necessitates effective goal-setting strategies. By setting intentional goals that reflect their core values and aspirations, individuals can navigate their paths with clarity and conviction. This process encourages a balanced approach to life, integrating work and personal aspirations in a way that promotes overall well-being. As individuals pursue their passions and align their actions with their purpose, they ultimately create a legacy that extends far beyond financial measures, contributing to a richer, more impactful existence.

Shifting Your Mindset for Abundance

Shifting your mindset for abundance begins with recognizing that your thoughts significantly influence your reality. When you cultivate a mindset centered on abundance, you become more attuned to opportunities that align with your purpose and passions. This shift involves moving away from a scarcity mentality, which often leads to fear and limitation, and embracing a perspective that sees potential and growth in every situation. By consciously choosing to focus on abundance, you open the door to innovative ideas, collaborations, and pathways that can transform your passion into a prosperous venture.

To effectively shift your mindset, it is essential to identify and challenge limiting beliefs that may hinder your progress. Many individuals carry subconscious narratives about money, success, and their own capabilities. These beliefs can stem from past experiences, societal conditioning, or comparisons with others.

Engaging in self-reflection can help you uncover these narratives. Once identified, you can replace them with empowering affirmations and beliefs that resonate with your true purpose. This process not only enhances your self-awareness but also builds a foundation for lasting change in your financial and personal life.

Practicing gratitude is another powerful tool in fostering an abundance mindset. By acknowledging and appreciating what you currently have, you create a positive feedback loop that attracts more of what you desire. Gratitude shifts your focus from what is lacking to what is already present in your life. This simple yet profound practice can help realign your energy towards your goals, making you more receptive to opportunities for growth and wealth creation. Incorporating daily gratitude rituals into your routine can enhance your overall emotional intelligence, enabling you to navigate challenges with resilience and clarity.

Surrounding yourself with a supportive community can further enhance your shift towards an abundance mindset. Engaging with like-minded individuals who share your passion for purposeful living and entrepreneurship can provide encouragement, inspiration, and accountability. These connections can serve as a catalyst for growth, allowing you to exchange ideas, collaborate on projects, and celebrate each other's successes. Building a network that values purpose-driven initiatives and personal growth fosters an environment where abundance thrives, reinforcing your commitment to achieving financial independence through passion projects.

Finally, embracing a proactive approach to goal setting can solidify your abundance mindset. Setting clear, purposeful goals aligned with your values and passions not only directs your focus but also motivates you to take actionable steps towards achieving them. Establishing milestones and celebrating small victories along the way reinforces a sense of accomplishment and progress. This practice not only nurtures your drive for success but also cultivates a sense of fulfillment that transcends monetary wealth. By integrating these strategies into your life, you empower yourself to not only discover your "why" but also to create a legacy of impact and abundance that resonates deeply within your community and beyond.

Overcoming Limiting Beliefs

Overcoming limiting beliefs is a crucial step in the journey towards discovering one's purpose and achieving true wealth in life. Limiting beliefs are the internal narratives that hold individuals back from realizing their full potential. These beliefs often stem from past experiences, societal expectations, or negative self-talk. Acknowledging and addressing these beliefs is essential for anyone looking to align their actions with their deeper values and passions. By recognizing that these beliefs are not inherent truths but rather perceptions shaped by circumstance, individuals can begin to challenge and redefine them.

To overcome limiting beliefs, the first step is to identify them. This can be achieved through self-reflection and mindfulness practices. Journaling can be particularly effective, as it allows individuals to articulate their thoughts and feelings, revealing patterns that may have gone unnoticed. Questions such as "What do I believe about my abilities?" or "What fears hold me back from pursuing my passions?" can provide insight into the beliefs that may be constraining personal growth. Once these beliefs are identified, individuals can start to assess their validity and explore their origins, which is vital for dismantling their power.

Transforming limiting beliefs requires a conscious effort to replace them with empowering affirmations. This process involves reprogramming the mind with positive statements that align with one's purpose and aspirations. For example, replacing "I am not skilled enough" with "I am continually growing and learning" shifts the focus from self-doubt to a more constructive mindset. Engaging in this practice daily can help reinforce a wealth mindset, encouraging individuals to embrace their unique strengths and capabilities. Surrounding oneself with supportive communities or mentors who embody a purpose-driven life can further reinforce these new beliefs.

Additionally, taking action is a powerful way to combat limiting beliefs. When individuals step outside their comfort zones and pursue activities that resonate with their passions, they gather experiences that challenge their doubts. Each small success builds confidence and demonstrates that the limiting beliefs were unfounded. Whether it's launching a passion project, engaging in purposeful living, or setting specific goals, these actions serve as proof that individuals can surpass their perceived limitations. This proactive approach fosters resilience and promotes a mindset geared toward growth and achievement.

Ultimately, overcoming limiting beliefs is integral to building a life of purpose and prosperity. It is a continuous journey that requires dedication, self-compassion, and the willingness to embrace change. By dismantling these barriers, individuals not only pave the way for personal fulfillment but also create the potential for financial independence and impactful legacy building. As one aligns their personal brand and identity with their true passions, they cultivate a life that reflects their values, leading to a more balanced and fulfilling existence.

Chapter 5: Personal Branding and Identity

Crafting Your Unique Brand

Crafting a unique brand begins with understanding the intricate connection between your personal identity and the purpose that drives you. Your brand is not merely a logo or a catchy tagline; it is the embodiment of your values, passions, and the impact you wish to create in the world. To effectively communicate who you are and what you stand for, you must first engage in deep self-reflection. Identify your core beliefs, strengths, and motivations that fuel your desire for a meaningful life. This introspective journey will form the foundation of your personal brand, allowing you to align your entrepreneurial endeavors with your authentic self.

Once you have a clear understanding of your identity, the next step is to articulate your unique value proposition. This involves defining how your passions translate into solutions that meet the needs and desires of your target audience. Consider what makes your approach distinct from others in your niche. Whether you are focused on wealth mindset coaching, purposeful living, or emotional intelligence, clarity in your value proposition will guide your messaging. It will help you communicate not just what you do, but why it matters, fostering a deeper connection with those who resonate with your vision.

In the digital age, personal branding extends beyond traditional marketing. It encompasses your online presence, social media interactions, and the content you create. Engaging storytelling is essential in sharing your journey, challenges, and triumphs. By showcasing your authentic self, you invite others to join you on your path. This transparency builds trust and loyalty among your audience, making them more likely to support your initiatives or invest in your services. Utilize various platforms to share insights that reflect your purpose, whether through blog posts, videos, or podcasts, ensuring that your voice is consistent and genuine.

Moreover, as you refine your brand, consider how it aligns with your financial goals and the legacy you wish to build. Purpose-driven entrepreneurship is not solely about profit; it's about creating value that contributes to your community and the world at large. Assess how your passions can lead to financial independence through projects that not only fulfill you but also create a positive impact. This integration of purpose and profit will not only distinguish you in your field but also attract like-minded individuals who share your vision, ultimately enhancing your network and opportunities.

Lastly, remember that personal branding is an evolving process. As you grow and your circumstances change, so too should your brand. Embrace the idea of continuous self-improvement and adaptability. Regularly revisit your goals and values, and be willing to pivot when necessary. This dynamic approach will ensure that your brand remains relevant and authentic, reflecting the wealth of purpose you cultivate in your life. By crafting a unique brand rooted in your passion and purpose, you set the stage for a fulfilling and prosperous journey that resonates with others seeking their own 'why.'

Aligning Your Brand with Your Purpose

Aligning your brand with your purpose is a transformative journey that begins with introspection and self-discovery. Understanding your core beliefs, values, and motivations is essential in crafting a brand that authentically reflects who you are. This alignment not only enhances your personal identity but also amplifies the message you want to convey to the world. When your brand resonates with your deeper purpose, it naturally attracts like-minded individuals who share your vision, fostering a community that supports your endeavors and amplifies your impact.

In the realm of purpose-driven entrepreneurship, aligning your brand with your purpose becomes a powerful strategy for sustainable growth. A business that embodies its founder's passion is more likely to thrive, as the energy and commitment behind the brand resonate with customers. This connection fosters loyalty and trust, which are critical components of long-term success. By clearly articulating your purpose within your branding efforts, you create a narrative that not only differentiates you from competitors but also inspires others to join your mission.

Financial independence through passion projects is another avenue where alignment plays a crucial role. When you pursue projects that are deeply connected to your purpose, you not only find fulfillment but also unlock new potential for wealth creation. This alignment allows you to channel your resources—time, energy, and finances—into ventures that resonate with your values. As you build your brand around your passion, you pave the way for opportunities that align with your vision of financial and personal success, ultimately leading to a more prosperous and meaningful life.

Personal branding and identity are also enhanced when you align your brand with your purpose. A strong personal brand rooted in authenticity attracts opportunities that are consistent with your values and aspirations. As you refine your brand message to reflect your purpose, you develop a clear identity that resonates with others, making it easier to form connections and collaborations. This clarity not only boosts your confidence but also positions you as a thought leader in your niche, empowering you to influence and inspire others on their own journeys.

Lastly, the journey of aligning your brand with your purpose is integral to legacy building and impact investing. When your brand embodies your core values, it creates a lasting impact that extends beyond financial gain. A purpose-driven approach to branding encourages you to consider the broader implications of your work and how it contributes to society. By focusing on creating value that aligns with your purpose, you set the foundation for a legacy that reflects your impact and inspires future generations to pursue their own paths of purpose and prosperity. This holistic view fosters a sense of fulfillment, ensuring that your work not only generates wealth but also enriches the lives of others.

The Impact of Authenticity on Success

Authenticity serves as a cornerstone for success, particularly for those seeking to uncover their purpose in life. In a world inundated with superficiality, the ability to remain true to oneself can distinguish individuals who thrive from those who merely exist. Authenticity fosters a sense of trust and loyalty, both in personal and professional relationships. When individuals align their actions with their core beliefs and values, they create a magnetic presence that attracts like-minded people, opportunities, and resources. This alignment not only enhances personal fulfillment but also lays the groundwork for lasting success.

In the realm of purpose-driven entrepreneurship, authenticity plays a vital role in brand identity. Entrepreneurs who embody their genuine selves in their business endeavors often resonate more deeply with their target audience. When customers perceive a brand as authentic, they are more likely to invest their time, energy, and money into it. This connection is particularly crucial in today's market, where consumers increasingly seek brands that reflect their values and beliefs. Therefore, crafting a personal brand that is grounded in authenticity can be a powerful strategy for building a loyal customer base and achieving sustainable growth.

Moreover, authenticity encourages emotional intelligence, which is essential for effective leadership and teamwork. Leaders who exhibit genuine behavior create environments where team members feel safe to express their ideas and emotions. This openness fosters collaboration, innovation, and resilience, all of which are critical components of a successful organization. When individuals recognize their own values and embrace their authentic selves, they can better understand and empathize with others, leading to stronger relationships and improved communication. This emotional intelligence not only enhances workplace dynamics but also contributes to an overall sense of well-being and fulfillment.

The journey toward financial independence is often driven by passion projects that align with one's authentic self. When individuals pursue ventures that genuinely resonate with them, they are more likely to put in the effort and dedication required to succeed. This intrinsic motivation can lead to innovative ideas, creative solutions, and a unique approach to problem-solving. Furthermore, the pursuit of passion projects can provide a sense of purpose that transcends monetary gain, ultimately leading to greater satisfaction in life. By focusing on what truly matters to them, individuals can create pathways to financial independence that are both rewarding and sustainable.

Finally, embracing authenticity allows individuals to contribute meaningfully to their communities and create a lasting legacy. When people live in alignment with their true selves, their actions reflect their values and passions, leading to impactful contributions. This alignment not only enriches their own lives but also inspires others to pursue their purposes. In this way, authenticity becomes a catalyst for positive change, encouraging a ripple effect that can transform communities and society as a whole. By prioritizing authenticity, individuals can build a legacy that resonates with their core beliefs, ultimately leaving a profound impact on future generations.

Chapter 6: Purposeful Living and Minimalism

Defining Minimalism in the Context of Purpose

Minimalism, when viewed through the lens of purpose, transcends mere simplicity and becomes a powerful catalyst for personal growth and fulfillment. At its core, minimalism is about stripping away the distractions and excess that cloud our vision, allowing us to focus on what truly matters in our lives. This focus facilitates a deeper understanding of our passions and motivations, ultimately leading us to discover our "why." By consciously choosing to eliminate the non-essential, we create space for reflection, enabling us to align our daily actions with our core values and aspirations.

In the context of purpose-driven entrepreneurship, minimalism serves as a guiding principle that encourages individuals to develop businesses that are not only financially viable but also resonate with their personal beliefs. Entrepreneurs who embrace a minimalist approach often prioritize quality over quantity, seeking to create impactful products or services that reflect their unique vision. This intentionality not only attracts customers who share similar values but also fosters a sense of authenticity and fulfillment in the entrepreneur's journey. By integrating minimalism into their business practices, these individuals can cultivate a sustainable model that aligns profit with purpose.

The wealth mindset is significantly enhanced by minimalism, as it shifts the focus from accumulating material possessions to embracing the richness of experiences and relationships. Those seeking financial independence through passion projects often find that a minimalist lifestyle allows them to allocate their time and resources more effectively. By identifying and pursuing activities that bring genuine joy and satisfaction, individuals can break free from the conventional definitions of success that often lead to burnout and dissatisfaction. This mindset fosters a sense of emotional intelligence, empowering individuals to make choices that enhance their overall well-being and financial stability.

Personal branding and identity are also influenced by the principles of minimalism. In a world saturated with information and choices, cultivating a clear and authentic personal brand becomes essential. Minimalism encourages individuals to distill their message and identity down to their core values and mission. This clarity not only helps in building a strong personal brand but also in establishing connections with others who resonate with that message. By focusing on what truly defines them, individuals can create a lasting impact and legacy that reflects their purpose and contributions to the community.

Ultimately, purposeful living and minimalism are intertwined in a way that fosters a balanced and fulfilling life. By embracing a minimalist philosophy, individuals can prioritize their goals and aspirations, leading to a greater sense of achievement and personal satisfaction. This lifestyle invites continuous reflection and growth, empowering individuals to design a life that is not only financially rewarding but also rich in meaning. By understanding minimalism in the context of purpose, one can embark on a transformative journey toward personal and financial fulfillment, leaving a legacy that inspires others to pursue their own passions and purpose.

The Benefits of Simplifying Your Life

The journey toward discovering your purpose often requires a thorough examination of your current life structure. Simplifying your life is a powerful strategy that can help clarify your values and priorities, ultimately guiding you toward a more purposeful existence. When you strip away the distractions and unnecessary complexities, you create space for what truly matters. This clarity can lead to a deeper understanding of your "why," allowing you to align your actions with your core beliefs and passions.

One of the most significant benefits of simplifying your life is the reduction of stress and anxiety. In a world that often glorifies busyness, many individuals find themselves overwhelmed by commitments and obligations that do not contribute to their overall happiness or purpose. By consciously choosing to eliminate non-essential tasks and distractions, you foster an environment where you can focus on your goals and passions. This shift not only enhances your emotional well-being but also boosts your productivity, as you direct your energy toward what truly matters.

Embracing a minimalist lifestyle encourages intentionality, a critical component of purposeful living. When you simplify your surroundings and commitments, you begin to make more thoughtful decisions regarding your time, resources, and relationships. This intentional approach allows you to cultivate a personal brand that reflects your authentic self, enhancing your identity and connecting you to your passions more deeply. As you develop a clearer sense of who you are, you become better equipped to pursue opportunities that resonate with your values, leading to greater fulfillment in both your personal and professional life.

Financial independence is a powerful motivator for many on the path to discovering their purpose. By simplifying your life, you can minimize expenses, declutter your financial commitments, and focus on passion projects that align with your interests. This approach not only fosters a wealth mindset but also creates opportunities for impact investing and legacy building. As you redirect your resources toward endeavors that reflect your values, you position yourself to create lasting change, not just for yourself but for your community and future generations.

Ultimately, simplifying your life is an act of self-awareness and growth. It allows you to prioritize emotional intelligence, which in turn enhances your ability to connect with others and navigate the complexities of personal and professional relationships. By fostering a balanced and fulfilling life, you can achieve not only wealth in a financial sense but also spiritual wealth and personal growth. As you embark on this journey, remember that each step toward simplification is a step toward uncovering your true purpose and embracing the wealth that comes with living authentically.

Creating a Purposeful Environment

Creating a purposeful environment is essential for individuals seeking to uncover their "why" in life. A purposeful environment fosters clarity, motivation, and the right mindset to pursue one's passions. This environment begins with the physical spaces we inhabit. Decluttering our surroundings not only minimizes distractions but also creates a sense of peace and focus. By surrounding ourselves with items that inspire us or represent our goals, we cultivate a space that aligns with our personal values and aspirations. This intentional design can serve as a daily reminder of our purpose, encouraging us to engage deeply with our passions.

Beyond physical space, the people we interact with significantly influence our journey toward discovering our purpose. Building a community of like-minded individuals who share similar goals and values can provide support and encouragement. Engaging with mentors or joining groups focused on personal development can enhance your understanding of purpose-driven entrepreneurship. These relationships create an atmosphere of accountability, where individuals can share insights, challenges, and successes, further solidifying their commitment to their personal journeys.

Embracing a mindset of abundance is another critical component of creating a purposeful environment. This mindset encourages individuals to view challenges as opportunities for growth rather than obstacles. Adopting practices such as gratitude journaling can enhance emotional intelligence, allowing individuals to recognize and appreciate the wealth of experiences around them. The belief that there is enough opportunity for everyone can foster collaboration and innovation, ultimately leading to financial independence through passion projects.

In addition to cultivating physical and social spaces, integrating purposeful living into daily routines is vital. This might involve setting aside time for reflection, goal setting, and aligning daily activities with long-term objectives. Incorporating minimalism into this routine can further streamline life, ensuring that time and energy are focused on what truly matters. By prioritizing activities that resonate with one's core values, individuals can create a sustainable work-life balance that not only enhances fulfillment but also amplifies their drive towards achieving their goals.

Lastly, legacy building is an integral aspect of a purposeful environment. Individuals seeking their "why" should consider the impact they wish to have on others and the world around them. This perspective encourages a long-term view of success that goes beyond personal gain, aligning financial independence with a greater mission. By investing in projects that resonate with their values and contribute to societal well-being, individuals can create a meaningful legacy that reflects their purpose, ensuring that their journey not only enriches their own lives but also leaves a lasting impact on future generations.

Chapter 7: Financial Independence through Passion Projects

Identifying Viable Passion Projects

Identifying viable passion projects begins with introspection and self-awareness. It is essential to assess your interests, values, and skills to pinpoint what truly resonates with you. This process often involves reflecting on moments when you felt most fulfilled or excited. Consider the activities that engage your mind and spirit, as these can serve as indicators of your genuine passions. By documenting these experiences and emotions, you create a reference point that can guide you toward projects that align with your core values and aspirations.

Once you have a clearer understanding of your passions, the next step is to evaluate their viability in the context of purpose-driven entrepreneurship. This involves exploring how your passions can solve problems or meet needs within your community or industry. Ask yourself critical questions: Is there a market for your passion? Who would benefit from it? By conducting research and seeking feedback from potential users or clients, you can assess whether your idea holds promise. This validation process helps ensure that your passion project not only brings personal satisfaction but also has the potential to create value for others.

Another vital aspect of identifying viable passion projects is aligning them with your long-term goals and financial aspirations. While pursuing your passion is important, it is equally essential to consider how these projects can contribute to your financial independence. Explore ways to monetize your ideas without compromising their essence. This might include developing products, offering services, or creating content that reflects your passion. By strategically planning how to integrate your passions into a sustainable business model, you can foster a mindset that embraces both personal fulfillment and financial success.

As you refine your passion project, developing a personal brand becomes crucial. Your brand should authentically communicate who you are and what you stand for. This process involves crafting a compelling narrative that highlights your journey, values, and the impact you wish to make. A strong personal brand not only helps in attracting an audience but also enhances your credibility and establishes trust. By sharing your story and engaging with your community, you create a supportive network that can provide encouragement and resources as you bring your passion project to life.

Finally, identifying viable passion projects requires a commitment to ongoing learning and growth. Embrace a mindset of adaptability, as the journey may lead you to unexpected opportunities and challenges. Set realistic goals and implement strategies for achievement, ensuring that you remain aligned with your purpose throughout the process. By fostering emotional intelligence and resilience, you equip yourself to navigate the complexities of entrepreneurship while maintaining work-life balance and fulfillment. Ultimately, the pursuit of a passion project should be a transformative journey that not only enriches your life but also contributes to a legacy of impact and inspiration for others.

Strategies for Monetizing Your Passions

Monetizing your passions begins with a deep understanding of what drives you and how that can translate into a sustainable income. The first strategy is to identify your core passions and align them with market needs. This involves conducting thorough research to understand what problems your passions can solve or what unique value they can provide to potential customers. Create a list of your interests, skills, and experiences, and then analyze which of these can be packaged into a product or service. This alignment not only increases your chances of success but also ensures that your work remains fulfilling and connected to your personal purpose.

Once you have identified a viable market opportunity, the next step is to build a personal brand that reflects your values and mission. A strong personal brand communicates authenticity and trust, which are essential in attracting an audience that resonates with your purpose. Utilize social media platforms and content marketing to share your journey, insights, and the unique perspective you bring to your niche. Engaging storytelling can help establish an emotional connection with your audience, making them more likely to support your endeavors. Remember, your brand is not just about what you do but also about who you are and the impact you want to make.

Creating multiple income streams is another effective strategy for monetizing your passions. Rather than relying solely on one source of income, diversify your offerings to include various products, services, or experiences. For example, if your passion lies in fitness, consider offering personal training sessions, online courses, merchandise, or even a subscription-based community. This not only increases your earning potential but also provides more opportunities to engage with your audience and fulfill their needs. As you explore different avenues, keep in mind the importance of maintaining a balance between your professional endeavors and personal well-being.

Networking and collaboration play crucial roles in the journey of monetizing your passions. Surrounding yourself with like-minded individuals can provide valuable insights, support, and opportunities for growth. Attend workshops, seminars, and events related to your niche to connect with others who share your vision. Collaboration can take many forms, from co-hosting workshops to partnering on projects that align with both parties' missions. These partnerships can expand your reach, enhance your credibility, and open doors to new opportunities that might not be accessible on your own.

Finally, maintaining a wealth mindset is essential as you pursue the monetization of your passions. This involves cultivating a belief in your ability to succeed and recognizing the value of your unique contributions. Embrace a mindset of abundance rather than scarcity, understanding that your success does not diminish the potential of others. Set clear, achievable goals and regularly assess your progress, celebrating milestones along the way. By fostering a positive relationship with wealth and success, you empower yourself to create a fulfilling life that reflects your passions, ultimately leading to financial independence and a lasting impact on the world around you.

Balancing Passion Projects with Financial Goals

Balancing passion projects with financial goals is a crucial endeavor for those seeking a fulfilling life aligned with their core values. Passion projects often stem from a deep-seated desire to express oneself, create meaningful work, or contribute to a cause. However, when these pursuits are not aligned with financial realities, they can lead to frustration or burnout, undermining the very purpose they were meant to serve. To navigate this balance, individuals must develop a clear understanding of their financial needs while remaining committed to their passions.

The first step in balancing these two aspects is defining what success looks like in both realms. Financial goals often include targets like savings, investments, and income generation, while passion projects focus on personal fulfillment, creative expression, or community impact. By establishing specific, measurable objectives for both areas, individuals can create a roadmap that integrates their passion-driven pursuits with their financial aspirations. This clarity enables them to make informed decisions about where to allocate their time, energy, and resources.

Time management plays a pivotal role in achieving this balance. Individuals should carve out dedicated time slots for their passion projects while also prioritizing their financial responsibilities. This structured approach allows for focused work on projects that ignite their enthusiasm without neglecting income-generating activities. Setting boundaries around work hours, personal time, and project work helps in maintaining a healthy equilibrium, ensuring that neither passion nor financial goals overshadow the other.

Moreover, leveraging skills acquired through passion projects can enhance financial prospects. For instance, a passion for writing can lead to freelance opportunities or content creation that generates income. By viewing passion projects through the lens of skill development, individuals can transform their creative endeavors into viable financial opportunities. This synergistic approach not only fosters personal growth but also contributes to long-term financial stability, reinforcing the idea that pursuing one's passions can indeed lead to prosperity.

Ultimately, the journey of balancing passion projects with financial goals requires a mindset grounded in purpose and resilience. Individuals must remain adaptable, recognizing that the path to financial independence through passion may not always follow a straight line. Embracing setbacks as learning opportunities and celebrating small victories along the way can sustain motivation and reinforce the connection between purpose and prosperity. In doing so, they can create a legacy that reflects their values while achieving the financial independence that allows their passions to flourish.

Chapter 8: Spiritual Wealth and Personal Growth

The Intersection of Spirituality and Wealth

The intersection of spirituality and wealth is a profound area of exploration for those seeking to understand their purpose in life. Many individuals often perceive wealth solely in material terms, equating financial success with happiness. However, this narrow view neglects the deeper aspects of what it means to be truly prosperous. Spirituality invites us to consider wealth not just as a financial metric, but as a holistic concept that encompasses emotional, mental, and spiritual well-being. By recognizing this broader definition, individuals can align their financial pursuits with their inner values, leading to a more meaningful and fulfilling life.

Purpose-driven entrepreneurship exemplifies how spirituality and wealth can coexist. Entrepreneurs who operate from a place of passion and purpose are often more resilient and innovative. They create businesses that reflect their values and contribute positively to society. This alignment not only enhances their personal brand but also attracts like-minded customers who resonate with their mission. In this way, the pursuit of financial success becomes a vehicle for personal expression and communal impact, reinforcing the idea that true wealth is derived from fulfilling one's purpose.

Moreover, cultivating a wealth mindset involves integrating spiritual principles into financial planning and goal setting. Individuals can benefit from practices such as gratitude, mindfulness, and visualization, which enhance emotional intelligence and resilience. These practices encourage a deeper understanding of one's motivations and aspirations, allowing for the creation of goals that are meaningful rather than merely profitable. By fostering an abundance mentality, individuals can shift their focus from scarcity to opportunity, making space for more fulfilling and impactful projects that resonate with their core values.

Financial independence through passion projects is another manifestation of the synergy between spirituality and wealth. When individuals engage in work that aligns with their passions, they not only find fulfillment but also unlock new avenues for financial growth. Passion projects often stem from a desire to serve others or solve societal problems, leading to innovative solutions that can generate income. This approach not only empowers individuals to create wealth but also reinforces the idea that financial success can be achieved without compromising one's values or purpose.

Ultimately, the journey towards wealth and purpose culminates in legacy building and impact investing. Individuals who prioritize their spiritual growth and purpose are inclined to consider the long-term effects of their financial decisions on future generations. They seek to leave a lasting impact that transcends personal gain, focusing instead on how their actions contribute to the greater good. This perspective fosters a sense of fulfillment and connection, illustrating that the true wealth lies not just in what one accumulates but in the positive influence one has on the world around them.

Practices for Nurturing Spiritual Wealth

Practices for nurturing spiritual wealth are essential for individuals seeking to align their lives with a higher purpose. Spiritual wealth transcends material possessions and financial gains, anchoring individuals in values, beliefs, and a sense of belonging. To cultivate this type of wealth, one must engage in practices that foster self-reflection, gratitude, and connection to something greater than oneself. These practices can significantly enhance personal growth, clarify one's purpose, and ultimately lead to a more fulfilling life.

One effective practice is mindfulness meditation, which encourages individuals to become present with their thoughts and feelings. By dedicating time each day to sit quietly and observe the mind, individuals can uncover deeper insights about their motivations and desires. This practice not only reduces stress but also creates space for clarity regarding one's purpose. As individuals become more attuned to their inner selves, they can better identify their passions and how these can be translated into meaningful pursuits.

Gratitude journaling is another powerful tool for nurturing spiritual wealth. Taking time to acknowledge and appreciate the positive aspects of life can shift one's mindset from scarcity to abundance. By regularly recording things they are thankful for, individuals cultivate a sense of fulfillment and happiness. This practice reinforces the idea that wealth encompasses more than financial success; it includes the richness of experiences and relationships. Through gratitude, individuals can also deepen their connection to their purpose, as they recognize the contributions of others and the opportunities that have shaped their journey.

Engaging in community service or volunteer work can further enhance one's spiritual wealth. Contributing to the well-being of others creates a sense of connection and reinforces the notion that true wealth lies in giving back. Purpose-driven entrepreneurs often find that their most fulfilling projects emerge from a desire to serve their communities. By aligning personal passions with the needs of others, individuals can create impactful legacies while nurturing their own sense of purpose. This symbiotic relationship between service and personal growth can lead to profound transformations in both the giver and the receiver.

Finally, establishing a vision board can serve as a tangible representation of one's goals and aspirations. This creative practice allows individuals to visualize their ideal life and the steps necessary to achieve it. By regularly updating and reflecting on their vision board, individuals can remain focused on their purpose and adjust their actions as needed. This visual reminder not only enhances motivation but also reinforces the belief that spiritual wealth is within reach. As individuals pursue their passions and align their actions with their core values, they foster a life rich in meaning, fulfillment, and ultimately, prosperity.

Personal Growth as a Wealth Builder

Personal growth serves as a crucial foundation for building wealth, transcending the mere accumulation of financial resources. At its core, personal growth involves the continuous evolution of an individual's mindset, skills, and emotional intelligence. This transformation fosters a deeper understanding of one's purpose, enabling individuals to align their actions with their values and aspirations. By cultivating a wealth mindset, individuals can unlock the potential to turn their passions into profitable ventures, creating a life that is not only financially rewarding but also rich in meaning and satisfaction.

Purpose-driven entrepreneurship epitomizes the intersection of personal growth and financial success. Entrepreneurs who are deeply connected to their "why" are more likely to pursue ventures that resonate with their core values. This alignment leads to greater resilience in the face of challenges and a more profound commitment to their goals. By focusing on the motivations behind their business endeavors, these entrepreneurs can create unique offerings that not only meet market needs but also contribute positively to society. This approach not only enhances their financial prospects but also nurtures a sense of fulfillment, reinforcing the notion that wealth extends beyond monetary gains.

Developing a strong personal brand is an essential aspect of leveraging personal growth for wealth creation. A clear and authentic identity enables individuals to communicate their values and passions effectively, attracting opportunities that align with their purpose. By investing time in understanding and articulating their unique story, individuals can differentiate themselves in a crowded marketplace. This personal branding not only enhances visibility but also builds trust with potential clients and partners, fostering relationships that can lead to collaborative ventures and increased financial success.

Financial independence through passion projects is another manifestation of personal growth as a wealth builder. When individuals engage in projects that ignite their passion, they often find themselves more motivated and productive. This intrinsic motivation can lead to innovative ideas and solutions that capture market interest. Moreover, pursuing passion projects encourages a minimalist mindset, where the focus shifts from consumerism to meaningful engagement with one's work. This shift not only contributes to personal satisfaction but also promotes sustainable financial practices that lead to long-term wealth accumulation.

Lastly, personal growth fosters emotional intelligence, a vital component in the realm of wealth creation. Understanding and managing one's emotions, as well as empathizing with others, can significantly enhance personal and professional relationships. Strong emotional intelligence equips individuals with the tools to navigate challenges, build networks, and capitalize on opportunities. This relational wealth is invaluable, as it leads to collaborative partnerships and community support that can amplify financial success. Ultimately, as individuals prioritize personal growth, they lay the groundwork for a fulfilling life that harmonizes purpose and prosperity, reinforcing the belief that true wealth is a holistic experience.

Chapter 9: Goal Setting and Achievement Strategies

Setting Purpose-Driven Goals

Setting purpose-driven goals is fundamental for individuals seeking to uncover their "why" in life. Purpose-driven goals are not just about achieving success in a traditional sense; they are about aligning your aspirations with your core values and passions. When you set goals rooted in your purpose, you create a roadmap that guides you towards fulfillment and financial independence. This alignment fosters a sense of direction, making it easier to navigate the complexities of life and entrepreneurship while staying true to oneself.

To begin setting purpose-driven goals, it is essential to engage in deep self-reflection. Understanding what truly motivates you—your passions, strengths, and values—lays the groundwork for meaningful goal-setting. Ask yourself questions like: What activities bring me joy? What issues am I passionate about? What legacy do I want to leave behind? This introspection allows you to articulate your purpose clearly, serving as a compass that can guide your decisions, both personally and professionally. The clearer your understanding of your purpose, the more focused and impactful your goals will be.

Once you have a clear sense of purpose, it is crucial to translate that into actionable goals. This process involves breaking down your overarching purpose into specific, measurable, achievable, relevant, and time-bound (SMART) goals. For instance, if your purpose revolves around promoting financial literacy, a goal could be to conduct monthly workshops in your community. By setting such goals, you create tangible milestones that not only reflect your purpose but also provide a sense of accomplishment as you progress. This structure helps maintain motivation and commitment, essential components for long-term success.

Incorporating principles of emotional intelligence into your goal-setting process can enhance your ability to connect with others and foster collaboration. Understanding your own emotions and those of others can lead to more impactful and purpose-driven interactions. For example, when you align your goals with the needs of your community or audience, you amplify your impact. This approach not only advances your own objectives but also contributes to the collective well-being, reinforcing the notion that personal success is intertwined with the success of others.

Finally, purpose-driven goals should be revisited and refined regularly. Life is dynamic, and as you grow, so too may your understanding of your purpose. Regularly evaluating your goals ensures they remain relevant and aligned with your evolving identity. This practice supports a lifestyle of purposeful living, where you embrace minimalism by focusing on what truly matters, thus avoiding distractions that do not serve your mission. By committing to this iterative process, you not only build a legacy of impact but also cultivate a wealth mindset that thrives on continual personal growth and fulfillment.

Effective Strategies for Achieving Goals

Effective goal achievement requires a clear understanding of your purpose, as this serves as the foundation for your aspirations. Defining your "why" is crucial; it acts as a compass, guiding your decisions and actions. When you align your goals with your core values and passions, the journey toward achievement becomes more meaningful and motivating. Take the time to reflect on what truly matters to you. This self-discovery process can illuminate the path to your goals, ensuring that they resonate with your identity and contribute to your overall sense of fulfillment.

Once you have established your purpose, the next effective strategy is to set SMART goals—Specific, Measurable, Achievable, Relevant, and Time-bound.

This framework provides clarity and structure, making it easier to track your progress and stay accountable. For instance, instead of saying, "I want to be financially independent," you could state, "I will save $10,000 within the next year by reducing unnecessary expenses and increasing my income through freelance work." Such specificity not only clarifies your intentions but also creates a tangible roadmap to follow, transforming vague ambitions into actionable steps.

Another powerful strategy is to cultivate a growth mindset. Embracing challenges, learning from setbacks, and viewing failures as opportunities for growth are essential components of this mindset. When you approach your goals with resilience and adaptability, you are more likely to navigate obstacles effectively. Engage in continuous learning and seek feedback to refine your strategies. This not only enhances your skills but also keeps you motivated as you witness your progress. A growth mindset fosters an environment where setbacks do not deter your commitment but instead fuel your determination to succeed.

Support systems can significantly enhance your goal-achievement process. Surrounding yourself with like-minded individuals who share similar ambitions can create a sense of community and accountability. Whether through networking events, mastermind groups, or online forums, connecting with others who are also in pursuit of their passions can provide encouragement and inspiration. Additionally, consider seeking out mentors who have successfully navigated similar paths. Their insights can offer valuable guidance and help you avoid common pitfalls, accelerating your journey toward achieving your goals.

Finally, regularly evaluate and adjust your goals as necessary. Life is dynamic, and your aspirations may evolve as you gain new experiences and insights. Periodically revisiting your goals allows you to assess their relevance to your current situation and purpose. This reflective practice can help you stay aligned with your true self and make informed decisions about your future. By remaining flexible and open to change, you can ensure that your goal-setting process remains a powerful tool for personal growth and wealth creation, ultimately leading to a legacy that embodies your purpose.

The Role of Accountability in Success

Accountability plays a pivotal role in achieving success, especially for those seeking their purpose in life. When individuals identify their "why," they often encounter challenges that test their commitment to their goals. Accountability serves as a fundamental mechanism to navigate these challenges, ensuring that individuals remain focused and dedicated to their passions. By establishing a system of accountability, whether through personal networks, mentors, or self-imposed structures, individuals can transform their aspirations into tangible outcomes, creating a direct link between purpose and achievement.

In the realm of purpose-driven entrepreneurship, accountability fosters a culture of responsibility. Entrepreneurs who hold themselves accountable are more likely to set realistic goals and create actionable plans to reach them. This proactive approach not only enhances their productivity but also nurtures resilience in the face of setbacks. By regularly assessing their progress and adjusting their strategies based on feedback, these entrepreneurs can stay aligned with their core values and mission. This alignment is crucial, as it ensures that their business endeavors reflect their personal identity and goals, ultimately leading to a more fulfilling and prosperous journey.

Personal branding and identity significantly benefit from accountability as well. When individuals commit to their unique narratives and values, they cultivate authenticity in their personal brands. Accountability helps maintain this authenticity by encouraging individuals to stay true to their vision and resist external pressures that may lead them astray. Regularly evaluating their actions against their values allows individuals to refine their branding efforts and ensure that their public persona resonates with their true selves. This alignment not only enhances their credibility but also attracts opportunities that are in harmony with their purpose-driven goals.

Furthermore, the concept of financial independence through passion projects is inherently tied to accountability. Individuals who pursue their passions often face uncertainty and risk, making it essential to adopt a disciplined approach to accountability. By setting specific financial goals and tracking their progress, individuals can gauge the viability of their projects and make informed decisions about resource allocation. Accountability encourages a mindset of continuous improvement, enabling individuals to pivot when necessary while maintaining focus on their overarching purpose. In doing so, they can create sustainable pathways to financial independence that are both rewarding and aligned with their passions.

Finally, the impact of accountability extends to emotional intelligence and personal growth. As individuals engage in self-reflection and seek feedback from others, they cultivate a deeper understanding of their strengths and weaknesses. This awareness is crucial for developing emotional intelligence, which plays a significant role in building meaningful relationships and achieving overall well-being. By holding themselves accountable, individuals can create a supportive environment that encourages growth, learning, and legacy building. Ultimately, embracing accountability not only enhances personal fulfillment but also empowers individuals to leave a lasting impact on their communities and the world.

Chapter 10: Legacy Building and Impact Investing

Understanding Legacy Beyond Financial Wealth

Understanding legacy requires a shift in perception from a narrow focus on financial wealth to a broader view that encompasses values, impact, and emotional richness. Financial wealth, often equated with success, represents only one facet of a person's life journey. True legacy transcends monetary assets; it is the sum of the relationships built, the values instilled, and the positive influence exerted on others. For individuals seeking their "why," recognizing that legacy is grounded in purpose leads to a deeper understanding of what it means to live a fulfilling life.

Purpose-driven entrepreneurship exemplifies how a business can serve as a vehicle for creating a meaningful legacy. Entrepreneurs who align their ventures with their core values and passions not only generate income but also contribute to societal change. This approach fosters a sense of fulfillment that financial success alone cannot provide. By focusing on what truly matters—solving problems, uplifting communities, and embodying personal beliefs—these individuals create businesses that reflect their identities and leave a lasting impression on the world.

Wealth mindset coaching plays a pivotal role in redefining legacy. It encourages individuals to cultivate an abundance mentality, which emphasizes the importance of giving back, sharing knowledge, and nurturing others. This mindset shift enables people to see wealth not just as a personal accumulation of resources but as a collective responsibility. By investing in personal growth and emotional intelligence, individuals can develop a legacy that resonates with their values, inspiring others to pursue their passions and contribute to a greater cause.

Personal branding and identity are crucial in shaping how one's legacy is perceived. Creating a strong personal brand that aligns with one's values and purpose helps communicate an individual's unique story to the world. This story can motivate others and create a ripple effect of positive change. A well-crafted legacy is not merely about what one achieves but how one is remembered. It encompasses the narratives we tell through our actions, our integrity, and the connections we forge with others. Therefore, individuals seeking their purpose should consider how they wish to be seen and the impact they want to leave behind.

Ultimately, the concept of legacy extends into various domains of life, including work-life balance, emotional intelligence, and purposeful living. Achieving fulfillment requires integrating personal values into daily practices, ensuring that one's actions align with their deeper motivations. Legacy building is not a solitary pursuit but a shared journey that influences and inspires others. As individuals explore their passions and strive for financial independence through purpose-driven endeavors, they discover that a rich legacy is created not just in what they leave behind, but in the lives they touch along the way.

Strategies for Impact Investing

Impact investing represents a powerful avenue for individuals seeking to align their financial pursuits with their core values and aspirations. By strategically allocating resources to ventures that generate both financial returns and positive social or environmental impacts, investors can create a legacy that reflects their purpose. The first strategy for effective impact investing is to clearly define personal values and goals. This foundational step involves self-reflection to identify what truly matters to you, whether it's sustainability, social justice, education, or healthcare. By grounding investment decisions in these values, individuals can pursue opportunities that resonate with their identity and contribute to their sense of purpose.

Another essential strategy is conducting thorough due diligence on potential investments. Understanding the social and environmental implications of an investment is critical to ensuring it aligns with one's values. This process includes researching the mission and impact metrics of organizations, assessing their track records, and evaluating how they measure success beyond financial returns. By prioritizing transparency and accountability, investors can select opportunities that genuinely contribute to societal well-being while also fostering personal fulfillment.

Networking with like-minded individuals and organizations can significantly enhance the impact of investment strategies. Engaging with communities focused on purpose-driven entrepreneurship and social innovation provides access to valuable insights and opportunities that may not be widely known. Collaborating with others who share similar passions can lead to innovative ideas, partnerships, and collective impact initiatives that amplify individual efforts. Building a network can also offer moral support and encouragement, reinforcing the notion that investing with purpose is both feasible and rewarding.

Incorporating a long-term perspective is another vital strategy for successful impact investing. While immediate financial returns are important, a commitment to sustainable development often requires patience and resilience. Investors should be prepared for potential fluctuations in financial performance and focus instead on the broader impact of their investments over time. By adopting a long-term mindset, individuals can pursue projects that may take years to yield significant social change while remaining aligned with their overarching purpose.

Finally, it is crucial to regularly evaluate and reflect on the outcomes of impact investments. This process involves not only assessing financial performance but also considering the social and environmental impact achieved. By analyzing successes and challenges, investors can refine their strategies, stay focused on their purpose, and adapt to changing circumstances. Continuous learning and adaptability are key components of effective impact investing, allowing individuals to evolve their approach as they grow in their personal journeys and deepen their understanding of how their investments can create meaningful change.

Creating a Lasting Legacy through Purpose

Creating a lasting legacy through purpose is a journey that begins with understanding the intrinsic motivations that guide your life. Identifying your "why" is crucial for establishing a foundation upon which you can build not just financial wealth, but a wealth of experiences, relationships, and contributions that resonate with your core values. A purpose-driven mindset allows you to navigate challenges with resilience and clarity, transforming obstacles into opportunities for growth. This clarity of purpose fuels passion, leading to endeavors that are personally fulfilling and impactful, both for yourself and the broader community.

Purpose-driven entrepreneurship embodies the essence of aligning your business pursuits with your core values and passions. By creating a venture that reflects your purpose, you not only enhance your own sense of fulfillment but also contribute positively to society. This alignment fosters genuine connections with customers and stakeholders, as they are often drawn to brands that resonate with their own beliefs and values. When entrepreneurs embed purpose into their business models, they create a sustainable framework that attracts loyal support and positions them as leaders in their respective fields.

Developing a wealth mindset is integral to creating a lasting legacy. This mindset goes beyond monetary wealth; it encompasses emotional, spiritual, and relational richness. Individuals who cultivate a wealth mindset recognize that their purpose fuels their ambition, motivating them to pursue initiatives that foster personal growth and community impact. Financial independence through passion projects becomes attainable when you leverage your unique skills and interests into ventures that align with your purpose. This approach not only leads to economic success but also ensures that your work is deeply satisfying and meaningful.

Personal branding and identity play significant roles in establishing a legacy rooted in purpose. Your brand is a reflection of who you are and what you stand for. By articulating your values and vision clearly, you attract like-minded individuals and opportunities that align with your purpose. This intentional branding helps you differentiate yourself in a crowded marketplace and reinforces your commitment to living authentically. As you build your identity around your purpose, you create a narrative that others can connect with, fostering community and collaboration.

Ultimately, creating a lasting legacy through purpose requires intentionality in goal setting and achievement strategies. By setting clear, purposeful goals, you can measure your progress and adjust your path as necessary. This focus not only enhances your productivity but also ensures that your efforts contribute to a larger vision of impact. Balancing work and life in pursuit of this legacy is essential; fulfillment comes from harmonizing your professional aspirations with personal well-being. By embracing emotional intelligence, you can navigate the complexities of relationships and decisions, ensuring that your legacy is one of integrity, compassion, and lasting influence.

Chapter 11: Work-Life Balance and Fulfillment

Defining Work-Life Balance

Defining work-life balance is essential for individuals seeking to align their personal aspirations with their professional endeavors. At its core, work-life balance refers to the equilibrium between the time and energy devoted to work-related activities and the time allocated for personal life, leisure, and self-care. This balance is crucial for fostering overall well-being, as it allows individuals to pursue their passions without sacrificing their health or relationships. For those exploring their "why" in life, understanding this concept is the first step toward creating a fulfilling existence that resonates with their core values and purpose.

Achieving work-life balance begins with self-awareness. Individuals must assess their current situation to identify what aspects of their lives require more attention. This involves reflecting on personal goals, values, and priorities. By recognizing what truly matters, individuals can set boundaries that protect their time and energy. It is important to differentiate between obligations and aspirations; the former often leads to burnout, while the latter fuels motivation and joy. Embracing this distinction allows for a more intentional approach to both personal and professional pursuits.

In the context of purpose-driven entrepreneurship, work-life balance becomes even more significant. Entrepreneurs are often passionate about their ventures, which can lead to an all-consuming focus on work. However, a sustainable business model thrives on the well-being of its creator. Balancing work and life helps maintain creativity and productivity, ensuring that the passion driving the business does not become a source of stress or disillusionment. By prioritizing self-care and personal interests alongside professional commitments, entrepreneurs can cultivate a richer, more rewarding experience.

Furthermore, work-life balance is intricately linked to emotional intelligence and wealth creation. Understanding one's emotions and recognizing the impact they have on decision-making can lead to better management of time and resources. Individuals with high emotional intelligence are more adept at navigating the demands of their careers while maintaining meaningful relationships outside of work. This balance contributes to a wealth mindset, where individuals view their resources holistically, leading to greater fulfillment and a deeper sense of purpose.

Ultimately, defining work-life balance is not merely about managing time but about creating a lifestyle that reflects one's values and aspirations. For those on a journey of personal growth and legacy building, this balance is fundamental. It allows for the integration of various life aspects, ensuring that personal fulfillment and professional success coexist harmoniously. By striving for this equilibrium, individuals can unlock their potential, transforming passion into prosperity while leaving a lasting impact on the world around them.

Strategies for Achieving Balance

Achieving balance in life is a multifaceted endeavor that requires intentional strategies centered around purpose. For individuals searching for their "why," it is essential to align daily activities with core values and passions. This alignment not only fosters a sense of fulfillment but also contributes to overall well-being. One effective strategy is the practice of self-reflection. Regularly assessing what matters most allows individuals to identify the activities that resonate with their true selves. By embracing a reflective mindset, people can prioritize their goals and eliminate distractions that lead them away from their purpose.

Another vital strategy is the establishment of boundaries. In a world that often glorifies busyness, learning to say no is crucial for maintaining balance. Individuals must recognize that their time and energy are finite resources. By setting clear boundaries around work, personal commitments, and leisure activities, one can create a structure that allows for focused engagement in areas that promote wealth and fulfillment. This practice not only protects one's time but also reinforces the commitment to living purposefully, allowing for deeper connections and more meaningful experiences.

Purpose-driven entrepreneurship offers a unique avenue for achieving balance by integrating passion with professional pursuits. Entrepreneurs can align their business objectives with their personal values, thereby creating a venture that not only generates income but also contributes to a larger mission. This approach fuels motivation and resilience, enabling individuals to navigate challenges with a sense of meaning. By focusing on projects that reflect their identity and aspirations, entrepreneurs can cultivate a wealth mindset that views success through the lens of impact rather than mere profit.

Emotional intelligence plays a significant role in balancing personal and professional life. Understanding one's emotions, as well as the emotions of others, can lead to more effective communication and relationship-building. This skill is instrumental in recognizing when to seek support or when to step back and recharge. By fostering emotional awareness, individuals are better equipped to manage stress, make informed decisions, and maintain harmonious relationships. As a result, emotional intelligence becomes a foundational element in achieving both personal growth and financial independence.

Lastly, goal setting serves as a roadmap for achieving balance. By establishing clear, purpose-driven goals, individuals can channel their energy into actionable steps that align with their values and aspirations. These goals should be specific, measurable, achievable, relevant, and time-bound (SMART), providing clarity and direction. Regularly revisiting and adjusting these goals ensures that they remain aligned with one's evolving purpose. Ultimately, by integrating these strategies—self-reflection, boundary setting, purpose-driven entrepreneurship, emotional intelligence, and goal setting—individuals can create a life that embodies balance, fulfillment, and lasting impact.

The Connection Between Purpose and Fulfillment

Understanding the connection between purpose and fulfillment is crucial for individuals seeking to uncover their "why" in life. Purpose acts as a guiding force, illuminating the path toward a more fulfilling existence. When people align their actions with their core values and passions, they experience a profound sense of satisfaction that transcends mere financial success. This alignment fosters resilience and motivates individuals to pursue their goals with determination, ultimately leading to a more meaningful life. By recognizing the intrinsic link between purpose and fulfillment, one can unlock the potential for both personal growth and financial prosperity.

Purpose-driven entrepreneurship exemplifies the powerful relationship between having a clear purpose and achieving fulfillment. Entrepreneurs who operate from a place of purpose are more likely to create businesses that resonate with their values and beliefs. This alignment not only attracts like-minded customers but also cultivates a loyal community that supports the brand. As these entrepreneurs pursue their passions, they often find that their work becomes an extension of their identity, enriching their lives and the lives of others. This synergy between purpose and entrepreneurial success highlights the potential for financial independence through passion projects.

A wealth mindset is an essential component of understanding the connection between purpose and fulfillment. Individuals who adopt a wealth mindset see opportunities where others may see obstacles. They recognize that true wealth is not solely measured by financial gain, but rather by the impact they make in their communities and the legacy they leave behind. This perspective encourages individuals to invest in their personal growth and to engage in purposeful living. By cultivating emotional intelligence, they can navigate challenges with grace and adapt their strategies to stay true to their purpose while achieving their financial goals.

Goal setting and achievement strategies play a pivotal role in bridging the gap between purpose and fulfillment. When individuals set goals that are aligned with their purpose, they are more likely to remain committed and motivated. The process of achieving these goals becomes not just about reaching a destination, but about the journey itself, enriching their lives in the process. By incorporating techniques such as visualization and mindfulness, individuals can enhance their focus and maintain a clear connection to their purpose. This approach not only fosters fulfillment but also encourages a sustainable work-life balance, allowing for a holistic approach to personal and professional development.

In the pursuit of legacy building and impact investing, the connection between purpose and fulfillment becomes even more pronounced. Individuals who prioritize their purpose in their financial decisions often find that their investments yield not only financial returns but also meaningful societal impact. This dual benefit reinforces the idea that wealth creation can be a vehicle for positive change. By aligning financial strategies with personal values, individuals can create a legacy that reflects their purpose, ensuring that their contributions resonate long after they are gone. In this way, the journey toward fulfillment becomes intertwined with the quest for a richer, more impactful life.

Chapter 12: Emotional Intelligence and Wealth Creation

The Role of Emotional Intelligence in Success

Emotional intelligence (EI) plays a crucial role in navigating the complexities of life and achieving success, particularly for those seeking to understand their purpose. At its core, EI encompasses the ability to recognize, understand, and manage our own emotions while also being attuned to the emotions of others.

This skill set is fundamental for anyone embarking on the journey of purpose-driven entrepreneurship, as it fosters the connection between personal values and professional endeavors. By cultivating emotional intelligence, individuals can forge deeper relationships, enhance communication, and create an environment conducive to collaboration and innovation, all of which are essential for building a meaningful and prosperous life.

Individuals with high emotional intelligence are often better equipped to identify their passions and align them with their goals. This alignment is crucial for those searching for their "why" in life. By understanding their emotional triggers and responses, they can discern what truly motivates them, leading to a more authentic expression of their identity and purpose. Moreover, emotional intelligence empowers individuals to navigate challenges with resilience and adaptability, allowing them to pivot when necessary and remain focused on their long-term objectives. This adaptability not only supports personal growth but also enhances the potential for financial independence through passion projects, as it encourages a mindset that embraces learning and development.

In the realm of personal branding and identity, emotional intelligence serves as a foundational element. A strong personal brand is built on authenticity, and EI helps individuals convey their true selves to the world. By being aware of their emotions and the emotions of others, individuals can craft a narrative that resonates deeply with their audience. This connection fosters trust and loyalty, which are vital components of a successful brand. As people increasingly seek relationships with brands that reflect their values, emotional intelligence becomes an invaluable asset for entrepreneurs and professionals alike, enabling them to create impactful and purpose-driven brands that stand out in a crowded marketplace.

Moreover, emotional intelligence is integral to achieving work-life balance and fulfillment. Those who are emotionally intelligent can better manage stress, communicate effectively with loved ones, and maintain healthy relationships, all of which contribute to overall well-being. By prioritizing emotional awareness, individuals can design a lifestyle that aligns with their values and aspirations, leading to greater satisfaction and a sense of purpose. This holistic approach not only enhances personal happiness but also positively impacts professional success, as fulfilled individuals are more likely to engage in their work passionately and creatively.

Finally, the connection between emotional intelligence and legacy building cannot be overlooked. Leaders who exhibit high EI are more likely to inspire others, fostering a culture of empathy and collaboration. As they build their legacy, these individuals create an impact that extends beyond their immediate achievements, influencing future generations. By integrating emotional intelligence into their purpose-driven journeys, individuals not only enhance their own success but also contribute to a richer, more compassionate society. This alignment of personal and communal values is a powerful driver of wealth creation, ensuring that success is measured not just in financial terms but also in the positive change one can effect in the world.

Developing Emotional Awareness

Developing emotional awareness is a foundational step for anyone seeking to uncover their purpose and achieve personal fulfillment. Emotional awareness involves recognizing, understanding, and managing one's emotions and the emotions of others. This skill is crucial for individuals on a journey to identify their "why" in life, as it helps connect personal values and passions with actionable goals. By cultivating emotional awareness, individuals can navigate their inner landscape, allowing them to discern what truly matters to them, thereby laying the groundwork for wealth in various forms—be it financial, spiritual, or relational.

To begin developing emotional awareness, individuals should practice self-reflection. This process involves taking time to contemplate one's feelings, motivations, and reactions to various situations. Journaling can be a powerful tool in this regard, as it encourages individuals to articulate their thoughts and emotions. Through writing, one can identify patterns and triggers that illuminate deeper desires and aspirations. This heightened self-understanding fosters a sense of clarity, enabling individuals to align their actions with their true purpose, ultimately driving them toward their goals.

Another vital component of emotional awareness is empathy. Empathy involves recognizing and understanding the emotions of others, which can significantly enhance personal branding and identity. By tuning into the feelings and needs of those around us, we can foster deeper connections and create a supportive community that resonates with our purpose. This connection not only enriches personal relationships but also opens doors to purposeful collaborations in entrepreneurial ventures. When entrepreneurs understand their target audience's emotions and desires, they are better equipped to create products or services that truly serve and impact others.

Furthermore, emotional awareness plays a critical role in work-life balance and fulfillment. When individuals are attuned to their emotional states, they can better manage stress and avoid burnout. Recognizing when to step back, recharge, or seek help can lead to a more sustainable approach to achieving personal and professional goals. This balance contributes to a holistic view of wealth, where emotional and mental well-being are regarded as equally important as financial success. By prioritizing emotional health, individuals can maintain focus on their passions and purpose, leading to a more fulfilling life experience.

Lastly, developing emotional awareness lays the groundwork for legacy building and impact investing. Individuals who are in tune with their emotions can better understand their long-term aspirations and the legacy they wish to leave behind. This insight empowers them to make informed decisions that align with both personal values and societal impact. As such, emotional awareness not only enhances personal growth but also contributes to creating a more compassionate and purpose-driven world. By embracing this journey, individuals can transform their passions into prosperity, ultimately enriching their lives and the lives of others.

Leveraging Emotional Intelligence for Wealth

Emotional intelligence (EI) serves as a vital tool in the pursuit of wealth, particularly for those seeking to align their financial aspirations with their deeper purpose in life. Understanding and managing one's emotions, as well as recognizing and influencing the emotions of others, can enhance decision-making processes and interpersonal relationships. In the context of wealth creation, those with high emotional intelligence are better equipped to navigate the complexities of personal branding, entrepreneurship, and investment strategies. They can identify opportunities that resonate with their values, leading to ventures that are not only profitable but fulfilling.

For individuals exploring their "why," emotional intelligence offers a pathway to self-discovery. By developing self-awareness, they can clarify their passions and motivations, which in turn informs their financial goals. This clarity enables them to pursue ventures that reflect their true identity, fostering a sense of authenticity in their work. When people engage in activities that align with their core values, they are more likely to experience sustained motivation and resilience, critical components for achieving financial independence through passion projects.

Purpose-driven entrepreneurship thrives on the foundation of emotional intelligence. Entrepreneurs who can empathize with their target audience are more adept at tailoring their products and services to meet genuine needs. This empathetic approach not only enhances customer satisfaction but also builds brand loyalty. As a result, businesses that prioritize emotional intelligence in their operations often outperform competitors who neglect this crucial aspect. For aspiring entrepreneurs, integrating EI into their business strategy can lead to both financial success and a meaningful impact on their communities.

Moreover, cultivating emotional intelligence can significantly influence one's approach to work-life balance and fulfillment. Individuals who recognize the importance of managing stress and maintaining positive relationships are more likely to experience greater job satisfaction and personal well-being. This balance is essential in preventing burnout and ensuring that the pursuit of financial goals does not overshadow personal growth and happiness. By fostering emotional intelligence, individuals can create a life that is not only prosperous but also rich in purpose and joy.

Finally, the legacy one leaves behind is often shaped by emotional intelligence. Those who understand the significance of their impact on others are better positioned to engage in legacy building and impact investing. By aligning their financial decisions with their values, they can contribute to causes that resonate with their purpose, creating a ripple effect of positive change. This approach not only secures financial prosperity but also fulfills a deeper desire to make a meaningful contribution to society, ultimately enriching both the individual and the community at large.

Chapter 13: Building Your Purpose-Driven Community

The Importance of Community Support

Community support plays a vital role in the journey toward discovering one's purpose and achieving personal wealth.

In the context of purpose-driven entrepreneurship, having a network of like-minded individuals can provide not only emotional encouragement but also practical resources and insights. When people share their experiences and challenges, it fosters an environment where ideas can flourish, and individuals can feel less isolated in their pursuit of passion projects. This supportive ecosystem can serve as a catalyst for personal growth, encouraging individuals to step outside their comfort zones and take the necessary risks to align their actions with their core values.

Building a strong community also enhances emotional intelligence, which is crucial for both personal development and wealth creation. Engaging with others allows individuals to practice empathy, active listening, and interpersonal communication. These skills are essential in the modern workforce, where collaboration and relationship-building are paramount. By interacting with diverse perspectives, individuals can deepen their understanding of themselves and others, which in turn enriches their sense of purpose. This emotional awareness can lead to better decision-making, helping individuals to navigate their entrepreneurial journeys with greater clarity and intention.

Additionally, community support often translates into opportunities for collaboration and partnership. When individuals come together with a shared vision, they can pool resources, skills, and networks to create innovative solutions and ventures. This collaborative spirit not only enhances the potential for financial independence but also encourages a mindset of abundance. In a community that celebrates collective achievements, individuals are more likely to view challenges as opportunities for growth rather than obstacles. This shift in perspective is crucial for those seeking to transform their passions into profitable ventures.

Moreover, a supportive community can serve as a source of accountability. When individuals articulate their goals and aspirations within a group, they are more likely to stay committed to their pursuits. The encouragement and constructive feedback from peers can motivate individuals to remain focused and resilient in the face of setbacks. This accountability is particularly important in the realm of goal setting and achievement strategies, where external support can provide the necessary nudge to keep individuals on track toward their objectives.

In conclusion, the importance of community support cannot be overstated for those searching for their "why" in life. It creates a nurturing environment where individuals can explore their passions, develop essential skills, and build meaningful relationships. This sense of belonging not only enhances personal and spiritual wealth but also lays the foundation for impactful legacy building. By engaging with a community that shares similar aspirations and values, individuals can enrich their journeys toward purposeful living and achieve a fulfilling work-life balance that aligns with their unique identities.

Networking with Purpose-Driven Individuals

Networking with purpose-driven individuals is a transformative experience that can significantly influence both personal and professional growth. When you engage with others who share a commitment to meaningful goals and values, you create a fertile ground for collaboration, inspiration, and mutual support. Purpose-driven networks often prioritize authentic connections over superficial interactions, leading to deeper relationships that can enhance your journey toward discovering your "why" in life. These relationships are built on shared aspirations, and they can help you clarify your vision, refine your goals, and maintain accountability in your pursuits.

In the realm of purpose-driven entrepreneurship, surrounding yourself with like-minded individuals can catalyze your ideas into actionable projects. Engaging with others who understand the nuances of aligning passion with purpose fosters an environment ripe for innovation. You can share insights, brainstorm solutions to challenges, and learn from the successes and failures of your peers. This collaborative energy not only fuels your entrepreneurial spirit but also encourages you to define and articulate your unique value proposition, enhancing your personal brand and identity in the process.

Moreover, networking with purpose-driven individuals allows for the exchange of wealth mindset coaching techniques that promote financial independence. By learning from those who have successfully turned their passions into profit, you gain access to strategies that transcend conventional business models. These individuals often emphasize the importance of aligning financial goals with personal values, reinforcing the idea that true wealth is not solely measured in monetary terms but also in the fulfillment and impact you generate. This holistic approach to financial independence encourages you to pursue passion projects that resonate with your core beliefs, creating a sustainable path to prosperity.

Purposeful living is further enhanced by the relationships formed within these networks. Interacting with others who prioritize work-life balance and fulfillment helps you to adopt practices that nourish your emotional intelligence and overall well-being. These connections provide opportunities for sharing experiences and strategies that lead to personal growth, allowing you to navigate the complexities of life with greater ease. By cultivating a mindset focused on living purposefully, you can achieve a sense of harmony between your ambitions and personal values, ultimately contributing to a more meaningful existence.

Finally, networking with purpose-driven individuals serves as a foundation for legacy building and impact investing. Engaging with those who are passionate about creating a positive change in the world can inspire you to consider the long-term effects of your actions. This mindset encourages you to think beyond immediate gains and focus on how your endeavors can contribute to a more equitable and sustainable future. As you connect with others committed to making a difference, you lay the groundwork for impactful projects that align with both your personal mission and broader societal needs, thus enriching your journey toward discovering your "why" in life.

Collaborative Projects for Shared Goals

Collaborative projects serve as a powerful avenue for individuals seeking to align their passions with shared goals, fostering a sense of purpose that can significantly enhance personal and collective wealth. Engaging in teamwork not only amplifies individual strengths but also cultivates a community that thrives on mutual support and shared objectives. This synergy is essential for those who are exploring their "why" in life, as it transforms solitary pursuits into a collective mission, enriching the experience and outcomes for all involved.

In the realm of purpose-driven entrepreneurship, collaborative projects can act as incubators for innovative ideas and solutions. When individuals come together, they bring unique perspectives and diverse skill sets that can lead to groundbreaking initiatives. These collaborations are often rooted in a shared vision, allowing participants to leverage each other's strengths while minimizing weaknesses. This environment of cooperation enhances not only creativity but also the drive to achieve meaningful results that resonate with the participants' values and aspirations.

Moreover, the emotional intelligence gained through collaborative efforts cannot be overstated. Working with others requires effective communication, empathy, and conflict resolution, all of which contribute to personal growth and a deeper understanding of oneself and others. This emotional growth aligns closely with the principles of purposeful living and minimalism—recognizing that personal fulfillment often stems from relationships and shared experiences rather than material possessions. As individuals learn to navigate interpersonal dynamics, they also refine their identities and personal brands in a way that is authentic and impactful.

Financial independence through passion projects can also be significantly enhanced by collaboration. By pooling resources and skills, individuals can embark on ventures that may have been unattainable alone. This shared approach to goal setting and achievement not only mitigates risks but often leads to greater financial rewards. When people unite their passions, they create projects that resonate with a wider audience, increasing the potential for success and financial sustainability. This collaborative mindset fosters a wealth-building culture that centers on purpose rather than mere profit.

Lastly, legacy building and impact investing are deeply enriched through collaborative initiatives. When individuals work together towards shared goals, they create a lasting impact that extends beyond personal achievements. This sense of community involvement and contribution to a greater cause can become a defining aspect of one's legacy. As participants engage in projects that reflect their values and passions, they not only fulfill their personal purposes but also inspire others, creating a ripple effect that fosters a wealth of purpose within society. Through collaboration, individuals can transform their passions into enduring legacies, ensuring that their contributions continue to resonate long after their efforts have concluded.

Chapter 14: The Journey of Continuous Growth

Embracing Change and Adaptability

Embracing change and adaptability is essential for anyone seeking to discover their "why" in life. Change is an inevitable aspect of existence, and those who resist it often find themselves stagnant or unfulfilled. In the pursuit of purpose, it becomes crucial to understand that flexibility allows individuals to navigate through life's uncertainties. When individuals learn to embrace change, they open themselves up to new possibilities and opportunities that align with their passions and values. This adaptability is a cornerstone of personal growth and is vital for anyone aiming to transform their passion into prosperity.

The journey of purpose-driven entrepreneurship necessitates a mindset that is open to change. As entrepreneurs strive to build businesses that reflect their values and passions, they will encounter various challenges and obstacles. Those who can pivot and adjust their strategies in response to market demands or personal experiences are more likely to succeed. This adaptability not only fosters resilience but also enhances creativity, allowing individuals to innovate and develop unique solutions that resonate with their purpose. By embracing change, entrepreneurs can refine their vision and ensure that their ventures remain aligned with their core values.

In the realm of personal branding and identity, adaptability plays a significant role in shaping how individuals present themselves to the world. As people grow and evolve, so too should their personal brands. Embracing change allows for the exploration of new facets of identity, which can lead to a more authentic representation of oneself. Individuals who are willing to evolve their messaging and branding strategies in response to their experiences and insights are better equipped to connect with their audience. This connection can enhance their impact and reach, ultimately contributing to their personal and financial success.

Financial independence through passion projects is a powerful concept that thrives on adaptability. Those who pursue their passions often face the need to adjust their plans and expectations as they learn more about themselves and the market. A willingness to embrace change enables individuals to explore diverse avenues for income, whether through side hustles, creative collaborations, or alternative business models. This flexibility not only enhances financial opportunities but also ensures that individuals remain engaged and motivated by their projects, fostering a sense of fulfillment that traditional paths may not provide.

Ultimately, embracing change and adaptability is essential for achieving a balanced and fulfilling life. As individuals work towards their goals, they must recognize that the path to purpose is rarely linear. The ability to adapt to life's twists and turns fosters emotional intelligence, enabling individuals to manage their reactions to challenges and uncertainties. This emotional resilience is a key component of wealth creation, as it allows individuals to remain focused on their purpose while navigating the complexities of life. By cultivating a mindset that embraces change, individuals can create lasting legacies and make meaningful contributions to their communities and the world at large.

Lifelong Learning as a Path to Wealth

Lifelong learning serves as a cornerstone in the journey toward wealth, not merely in financial terms, but also in personal fulfillment and purpose. Individuals seeking their "why" often find that continuous education—whether through formal channels, self-directed study, or experiential learning—enriches their understanding of themselves and the world around them. This ongoing quest for knowledge fuels personal growth, enhances emotional intelligence, and ultimately lays the groundwork for a wealth mindset. By fostering a habit of lifelong learning, individuals can cultivate a deeper awareness of their passions, allowing them to align their pursuits with their core values.

A wealth mindset is intrinsically linked to the principles of purpose-driven entrepreneurship. Entrepreneurs who commit to learning continuously are better equipped to adapt to changing markets and consumer needs. They develop resilience and creativity, enabling them to innovate and refine their offerings. As they grow in knowledge, they also gain confidence in their abilities, which empowers them to take calculated risks. This dynamic not only increases their chances of financial success but also ensures that their ventures resonate with their personal mission, creating a business model that reflects their identity and values.

Personal branding and identity play crucial roles in the path to wealth, and lifelong learning significantly enhances these aspects. As individuals explore various subjects and experiences, they begin to define their unique narratives. This process of self-discovery is essential in crafting a personal brand that stands out in an increasingly crowded marketplace. By embracing new knowledge and skills, individuals can articulate their purpose with clarity, making meaningful connections with others who share similar values. A strong personal brand rooted in authenticity can lead to opportunities that align with one's passions, ultimately resulting in both personal fulfillment and financial gain.

In the context of purposeful living and minimalism, lifelong learning encourages individuals to assess their priorities and eliminate distractions that do not serve their goals. Engaging in continuous education provides the tools to evaluate what is truly essential, leading to a more intentional life. This clarity fosters financial independence, as individuals become more discerning about their spending habits and investment choices. By focusing their resources on passion projects that align with their purpose, they can achieve a sustainable form of wealth that transcends material possessions and contributes to a legacy of impact.

Finally, the intersection of emotional intelligence and wealth creation cannot be overlooked. Lifelong learning enhances emotional intelligence by equipping individuals with the skills needed to navigate complex relationships and challenges. This capability is vital for building meaningful connections and fostering collaborations that lead to wealth, both materially and spiritually. As individuals grow in their emotional understanding, they become more adept at setting and achieving goals, contributing to their overall sense of fulfillment and success. In this way, lifelong learning is not just a pathway to wealth; it is a transformative journey that enriches one's life purpose and legacy.

Celebrating Your Progress and Future Goals

Celebrating your progress is an essential component of the journey toward realizing your purpose and achieving your goals. As you navigate the complexities of finding your "why," it's crucial to take a step back and acknowledge the milestones you have reached. Each step, no matter how small, contributes to your overall growth and development. Celebrating these achievements fosters a positive mindset and reinforces your commitment to your purpose. It serves as a reminder of your capabilities and encourages you to continue moving forward, even when faced with challenges.

Recognizing your progress can take many forms, from personal reflections to sharing your accomplishments with others. Consider keeping a journal to document your journey, noting not only your successes but also the lessons learned along the way. This practice not only helps you appreciate how far you've come but also provides a valuable resource for future reference. Sharing your story with a supportive community can amplify this effect, as others can offer encouragement and celebrate your successes alongside you, creating a sense of belonging that is vital for personal growth.

As you celebrate past achievements, it's equally important to look forward and set future goals. These goals should align with your identified purpose and reflect your aspirations for both personal and professional growth. The process of goal setting encourages you to clarify your vision and devise actionable steps to achieve it. By setting specific, measurable, achievable, relevant, and time-bound (SMART) goals, you can create a roadmap that guides your efforts and keeps you focused on your purpose. This structured approach transforms your passion into tangible outcomes, reinforcing the wealth mindset that is central to your journey.

Moreover, aligning your future goals with your core values ensures that your pursuits remain meaningful and fulfilling. As you define what success looks like for you, consider how your goals can contribute to not only your own well-being but also to the broader community. Impactful legacy building often begins with personal growth and the pursuit of passions that resonate deeply with your identity. By setting goals that reflect your values, you cultivate a sense of responsibility towards others, enhancing your emotional intelligence and enriching your path toward financial independence.

Ultimately, the act of celebrating progress and setting future goals encapsulates the essence of purposeful living. It encourages a balance between reflection and ambition, allowing you to appreciate where you are while remaining motivated to strive for more. This dynamic interplay between past and future creates a fulfilling journey that not only enriches your life but also inspires those around you. As you continue to embrace this cycle, you empower yourself to build a legacy that embodies your passions and purpose, leaving a lasting impact on the world.

Resources:

Take Your Wealth of Purpose to a Whole New Level:

https://www.wealthsquad.university/?via=KDP

www.ingramcontent.com/pod-product-compliance
Lightning Source LLC
Chambersburg PA
CBHW071023240526
45469CB00006BD/2058